CLOUD TRAIN

CLOUD TRAIN

Joan Aleshire

Texas Tech Press
Lubbock, Texas, U.S.A.
1982

Acknowledgments

Permission from the following to reprint the poems listed is gratefully acknowledged.

CommonWoman: "Georgia O'Keefe, as Photographed by Stieglitz"
Dark Horse: "Barnacle," "Just Looking at the Bones"
Firehouse: "The Amaranthine Desert," "The Disappeared Ones" (in an earlier version)
Intro: 12 "Barn Swallows," "To Mary Shelley"
Madog: "Coming Down Through the Fields" (in an earlier version)
Poetry Now: "The Concord String Quartet Plays Rutland High," "Family Man," "Immune to Spring"
Seattle Review: "The Dog's Breath"
Tendril: "Learning Not to Love You," "Museum of Natural History"
13th Moon: "Exhibition of Women Artists (1790-1900)," "Vermont Farm— 1890s"

Cloud Train, by Joan Aleshire, is published in cooperation with the Associated Writing Programs and is an *AWP Award Series Selection*.

ISBN 0-89672-098-5 (paper)
ISBN 0-89672-099-3 (cloth)
Library of Congress Catalog Card Number: 82-80305
Designed by Betty M. Johnson, set in Bookman Light,
printed on Texas Tech Opaque, 70 lb.
Texas Tech Press, Lubbock, Texas 79409
Copyright 1982 by Texas Tech University
Printed in the United States of America

Contents

For my teachers

1   Cloud Train

Cloud Train

You're working in the garden, ordinary
evening in early fall, covering tomatoes
against frost, when something stirs
in the western sky, and the garden
darkens. A mass of clouds crosses
the sunset, pushed by high winds
so it seems like a speeding train.

The sky blazes as if a city were
burning, and it seems that the train
escapes it, stops at no stations,
while startled linemen leap from the tracks.
Soldiers crouch on every car, shoulders
and helmets edged in gold.

The train fills the screen of sky
above you; you can almost hear
the clatter of wheels on track, feel
soot on your skin. It's like watching
a silent film with no end, only
a middle where danger always threatens,
where the only action is this relentless
dash toward the rim of trees. The soldiers'
hands reach down to you, almost strong enough
to pull you out of the garden, on board.

Grandmother and Great-Aunts

Rainy days in my grandmother's attic,
photographs fell from albums, cracked
as dry leaves. I studied the faces
of my grandmother and her three sisters,
hoping to find which was the rebel,
which read Greek, which was slow
but psychic, which died at eighteen.

Uniformly smooth and solemn, their faces
resisted me. In the only picture with a date,
all four are smiling, posed on a dock,
arms around each other's waists,
the hull of a sloop behind them.

I imagined them taking up sketch pads
as the captain tacked past the spice company
where black workers hoisted sacks of cinnamon,
past a mass burial for typhoid victims,
past the fish pier where cats fought
for rotting scraps, past the houses on the point
where their mother stood watching.

Remembering my grandmother's story,
I imagined how the wind died,
the captain let the mast swing out,
sheets dipping in the water.
The sisters snapped open their fans,
splashed salt water on their faces,
sweated in high lace collars.

The captain drew a bucket from the galley.
Elizabeth, defiant, ignored her sisters'
warning of typhoid, dared to take the dipper,
saw her own face rise to meet her, held
the clear, sweet-seeming water in her mouth
a moment, a lifetime.

Lungs

The last time I stayed with my grandmother
at the house in Maine she loved,
I was twenty and bored by the fog
that closed us in all August,
its hand at my grandmother's throat.

Asthma, emphysema: the words
seemed like her struggles for breath,
as I strained my ears to catch
the sound, breathing easier
when she did, both of us
turning back to our books.

Evenings we played backgammon,
her long, ringed fingers rattling
the ivory dice, moving pieces
as intently as if a fortune
were at stake. Or she'd gossip,
criticize the Kennedys, fierce,
fast-talking, scarcely slowed
by pauses for breath.

When I thought she was asleep,
I'd go out to meet a man I liked,
and once, guilty, inching home
through the fog, I found her awake,
long hair loose, its white turned yellow
in the light of the radio dial,
the delicate glass bowl of her atomizer
shining like a bottle before a ship
assembles itself inside.

Her breath was louder than her voice,
her gasp louder than breath—a shallow,
straining sound, like a rope wound
on a winch. The oxygen tank stood
in the corner like a warning. With each
intake of spray, her shoulders rose
as if she was shrugging. "Stay
with me," she breathed out; then
"This isn't bad," and the weight
on her chest lifted a little,
as though someone had decided:
"Not this time." The air flowed
freely into her tired lungs, out;
she ordered me to bed, my grandmother,
her voice clearer now. Only the faintest
chord like the strumming of a guitar,
like longing, lingered in her throat.

To My Mother

You worry because I live alone.
Something—but I don't know what,
because I shift the phone from ear
to ear—bad may happen. I should be
careful, or better, move back home.

After I hang up, my own expression
thrown back from the mirror reminds me
of a photograph of you at twelve.
Your hair, now so carefully curled,
was unruly as mine, escaping your hat.

You stood next to your pony, one
hand on his halter, the other
stroking his blazed nose. Impulse
to flight flickered in your smile;
I expect you cantered off bareback
just after the shutter closed.

My aunts say you were fearless
then, bent low to the pony's neck,
urging him to the highest fence, and
over it. When did you start
to be afraid? I think how doubt
like a falling leaf can flutter
at the corner of an eye. The pony,
once part of you, shifts like water;
the trees, once distinct at the edge
of the pasture, blur to make a wall.

The Dark Ages

Whenever you start to fall asleep
against the cold hearthstone, the rats
creep out and rummage for hard crumbs
of cornbread scattered under the table
from your last meal. You can hear their
claws on the chairs. The last log burned
yesterday; stone crocks stand bare
in the pantry. Snow has fallen for months,
and tonight is falling still. You take
the tapestry off the wall and wrap it
around you. Even the dogs that might have
lain across your feet have died. You miss
the sound of their snarling as they
quarrelled over bones in the great hall.

At first it seemed the usual winter's
rate of death, taking the grandfathers
and old cooks, infants and their mothers,
scouts shot in raids along the borders. Then
it seemed everyone began to cough, fiercely
at first, then weaker and weaker, until
you looked up from nursing your father—
and everyone was gone. The snow was falling still.

It seemed that spring should come, seemed
that time of year, though you had lost
all sense of days. Sometime as you watched
your father's face turn to marble, day
and night became the same. The pass is
filled with snow as high as the mountains.
Perhaps you will have to kill the rats,
who are getting bolder and tugging at the edges
of your sleep. In your dream, a lopsided
spring moon shines across the floor, scaring
the rats. There is a knock on the door, and
out of the dark, someone steps, smiling.

Vermont Farm—1890s

Once there was a woman
put plates on the table
with a sharp click, ladled stew
from the cookstove, stepped briskly,
lavender rising from her skirts.
Long wrists, long fingers deftly
handed round the relish, handed the butter
she had churned, sliced the bread
which fell firm and light.
The hired man's hand where she brushed it
was hot as the fire.

And her husband, tight and dour, brooded
on the back field full of boulders
big as sheep, worried over sickly calves,
scrawny cows, had not touched her
for a year, had not looked up as she
passed, grunted at the food.

Four children under five, foot
on the treadle, hand at the churn,
pressing the cheese. The hired man
notices her watching him; her hand
trembles as she passes his plate.
When she speaks, she's out of breath.

Woodheat cracks her hair, her skin.
The wool collar scratches her neck;
her stockings bite like ants.
One step from a scream, she unlatches
the door. There's nothing to see
but blank fields of snow
and the shape of her own breath in the cold.

Exhibition of Women Artists (1790-1900)

She painted in the kitchen
studying grapes and peaches,
a bowl of pears she later cut,
peeled and stewed for dinner.

Or these oranges arranged on black velvet:
a friend from the South must have brought them.
The velvet would become a daughter's dress
she'd spend the night sewing for Christmas.

Everything glows against the black:
the orange of oranges, white wax of blossoms.
The painting glows on this museum wall,
has come a long way from the easel
set up in the kitchen so the artist
could paint with one hand, cook with the other,
turn up her sleeve to test warm milk
against her skin, add sugar to taste,
soothe the colicky child tossing its cradle.

Onions, eggs, peppers, beans:
she studied shapes before she quartered them,
preserving their life with her brush.

Georgia O'Keefe, as Photographed by Stieglitz

When he shows her work in his gallery,
she comes to see how it's framed.
At first she might be any visitor,
posing once for Stieglitz. Her face soft,
she smiles to please, a nice young
teacher in a sensible suit, painting on the side.

Soon she spends the night.
In the morning, her hair is loose,
her face seems drugged. The sun's mouth
touches her throat, part of her breasts
where the kimono falls open.

Obsessed with her hands,
he poses them over and over
as sea stars or anemones.
Sometimes, in a fit of rage,
one starfish attacks another.
He never shows her cooking or painting;
even when she threads a needle,
he sees her hands as swans.

Nude, cropped at chin and knees,
she might be a goddess cast in bronze,
or, spreading her legs, the neighborhood
whore. But sometimes her breasts,
cradled by her arms, look translucent
and fragile as eggs.

Years or months later, he shows her
full-length, from a distance,
dressed in a dark cape, with a satisfied
smile. Her hands, now hard and competent,
stroke the hubcap of a shiny Ford V-8.
Her face, framed in the car window,
is whittled to a frown.

In the last picture, she seems
part of her own dark painting,
her black shape blending
with the shape in oil behind her.
She stares at the camera, calm
and severe as a nun, ready at last
to move out of range.

Women's Prison—1930s

All that's left of the women's prison
is a few photographs, a high, brick-faced
granite wall, three steps to the street,
and a marble walk that ends in grass.
As I drive past each week, I think of the women
sentenced to live there. What were
their crimes? Child-murder, robbery,
prostitution—would they be criminals now?

The laundry where they worked
was light, high-ceilinged. Pots of clothes
simmered like soup on the stove.
Sleeves rolled to the elbow, one woman
helps another hold sheets taut
through the mangle. A third turns
the crank, braided head circled in steam.

I imagine a prisoner who irons
for customers from town often holds
a silk blouse to her shoulders,
or measures a child's dress with her eyes.
Once in a while, someone rips a sheet
in half, someone screams, another stands
like a waxwork as the smell of scorched
cloth rises from a half-ironed blouse.

Though the street door isn't locked—
this is a "model prison"—no one
unlatches it. One prisoner pulls a sheet
from the pile where they've drifted;
another takes the opposite end. They snap
the sheet smooth, step together folding,
flipping, making a square in mid-air.

The steam that fills the room
washes away memories as it smooths
skin. Bare wood floors. Babies. Back
of a man's hand. Salesmen's jokes.
Shoes with cardboard soles. Hair curls
in the dampness; faces are flushed,
even smiling, over the work.

In the windy, sunlit yard, sheets
flap on the line like the wings
of large, tired birds, maybe snowgeese
headed south. Gathering the sheets
in baskets, the women carry them
inside, where they rest—masses
of white feathers, gaining strength,
as the women do, for the next long flight.

To Mary Shelley

One hot spring afternoon, crossing
from your bed to the window, you notice
a drop of blood on the marble floor.
One drop, as if you'd pricked your finger,
but you've been too tired to sew, too tired,
three months pregnant, to do much but sleep
while your friend Jane sings on the terrace
and Shelley rests his head on her knee.

You might ignore one drop,
but your body is heavy as if
an extra charge of gravity pulls you
to earth. I know how the pain begins:
it creases the small of your back,
then pulses like labor pain
though it's much too soon for birth.

And the blood, I know, becomes more
than a drop, is soon a warm river
down your legs, turning cold
as it soaks the sheets. Shelley,
more practical than you expected,
somehow finds ice in Italy, in spring,
and a metal tub where he holds you
as the river slows to a few pink swirls.

Only three months worth of cells—
scarcely a child—has died,
but you think death lives
in your body; you feel it
around you, and now whenever
Shelley stares at the bay, talks of sailing,
you see wave after wave
breaking in his eyes.

Barnacle

A woman alone in the country
peels off layers of long underwear,
peels down to her skin.
Mirrored in the double panes
of window-storm window, her waist
and thighs have the same denseness,
roundness as the trunks of black maples
in the snow, backlit by the moon.

Checking for changes, she feels
her belly and breasts: they seem
of the usual roundness, firmness,
but tonight she gains no pleasure
from the touch; it is an examination,
an exploration of a territory grown cold
and unfamiliar, her navel like a crater
on the moon.

Inside, a barnacle of cells has attached
itself to her life, her womb sounding
sharp notes of change. The barnacle
has fastened tight to the walls of her womb,
to the reaches of her mind.

It will grow; there's no way out
but pain. She spreads her fingers
across her belly: there will be
cold choices in the morning.

The Disappeared Ones

—for Diana

Your letter lies on my desk like
an outstretched hand I haven't touched
in years. It's summer here, winter
in Buenos Aires where you are, and where
the story I read was written. Pictures
of women you might know—who might be
you—beg for my attention. In coats
and gloves, they gather each Thursday
in the Plaza de Mayo, wearing photographs
around their necks like medallions,
holding enlargements up like flags.
The smiling faces are their husbands,
children, now listed as "missing,"
as if these thousands had run away
from home with new women, with
suitcases full of bills.

The tortures I read about don't need
illustration, each an electric shock
to the mind. The woman who lives to tell
how rats were put between her legs
was arrested on your street. I want
to ask if you're afraid, or if you ignore
the people who gather each Thursday
in the Plaza. What would I do,
if I lived there?

Now, as I try to write you, censors
stoke incinerators, add names
to lists. Questions I can't ask you
hang like weights on my pen. I stick
to the safety of memories, my family,
my work. And the women will meet
in the Plaza in thinner coats, then
in blouses, carrying their placards.
By now, though, these photographs
have begun to lie. If the disappeared ones
came back now, no one would recognize
them, except by noticing how the teeth
of skulls recall their smiles.

2   Museum of Natural History

Coming Down Through the Fields

As we come down through the fields,
the dandelions give way to buttercups.
The first daisies, purple clovers
leap from the feathery green.
These old meadows are steep grades;
the fight to clear them left no mark
on the grasses, as birds leave no tracings on air.

I hunt for wild strawberries on the south slope.
Tiny, shielded by leaves, ripe, unripe, pale:
I'll never find enough for jam or even dinner.
Your hips lurch right side up, left side down
as you climb down through the fields.
"Just eat them as you go," you say,
and the berries burst on our tongues.

The Curative Power of Garlic

Friends, as they say, for years
now, we talk of soil enrichment,
the life of stars, the curative
power of garlic. I memorize the veins
in his hands, pores of his skin, pattern
of his slightly crooked teeth.

Sold houses, lost friendships,
dreams slip into our talk
like spies. Sometimes it seems
we've jumped into a river,
the current of our voices
carrying us through pools deep
enough to drown in, to islands
only canoes have touched. Just
as we hear the roaring falls,
one of us takes hold of a branch.
On shore, we take different paths home.

Making dinner for my family, I find
the garlic turned to ivory, a tooth,
smooth stone peeled of its rosy skin.
I stare at the green shoot inside,
my eyes still so wide from taking in
his face that everything is magnified.

The Hair in the Sink

For months I ignore the signs
of betrayal: unexplained absences,
long apologies, a name he calls
in his sleep with more syllables
than mine. Then one night I find
a hair in the sink that wasn't
there that morning: jagged as
a crack, too long and dark
to be mine.

I suspect a break-in,
but the doors are intact,
drawers closed, stereo safe
on the shelf. There's nothing
on the bedspread, but I think
the sheets seem smoother
than I made them. Tearing the bed
apart, I find only my earring.

I've read that traumas
make hair grow this way:
like a drawing of lightning.
I imagine a woman who's been
through a lot, a woman I'd
like, or pity, brushing her hair
at my mirror. I think of
the man behind her—my husband.
She turns to him smiling, as
eagerly, helplessly, he takes
her shoulders in his hands and
one betraying hair falls in the sink.

I wrap the hair like a ring
round my finger, and wait.
I ready myself to meet him
like a fury, breath like a blowtorch
that could burn his eyes out.
But when I hear him at the door,
doubt closes its cold hand
on my throat. I think of
the woman at my mirror: is she
beautiful? Does my husband look
young again, meeting her there?

Museum of Natural History

1

Matchbooks from motels in the mountains
litter the table between us. Our angry
whispers wake the child, who blinks
in the doorway, "I'm having a dream."

We lie: "It's all right," and take turns
holding her, as we try not to notice how
she stares at us in the hard kitchen light.
Later I tell her, "Daddy's going to live
alone. In spring, you and I can move
to the country, have a pony and a garden."

2

We fill Sundays at the museum,
wandering the dim halls, drawn
to lighted displays of Indian life:
mothers teaching daughters to grind corn,
sons helping fathers skin a deer.

My daughter presses her nose
to the glass, and as her lips move,
I guess she imagines herself
paddling an Algonquin canoe.

I go back to the stuffed birds
building nests on a cliff in the next hall.
The plaque assures me the eggs they lay
are pear-shaped, will balance
in all but the strongest wind.

3

Like the Indians we study, we practice
survival: how to dial the police, cross
the street. The first time she steps
off the curb with the green light,
she looks stiffly right, left, glances
at the silver bulldog on a truck
that seems inches from her head.

When she reaches the far curbstone,
she doesn't look back, seems to grow
larger as she hurries to school. I wait
on the stoop for the scream of brakes,
my fear like a net I'll throw again
and again, forgetting it always falls short.

Planting Season

New leaves change the landscape.
Old farms, broken into house lots,
sprout surveyors' fluorescent flags.
Friends, splitting up, store books
in our attic, as if we'll never move.
Their houses, where we once were warm,
fill with strangers or stand darkened now.

Spring always rushes us,
though we've waited so long. Unlike
our neighbors, gardens in by now,
we haven't plowed or talked of planting.
I'm afraid to ask, and find you're leaving,
toothbrush permanently in your pocket,
hiking boots on, even in bed.

Lifting straw from the herbs,
I see only sage survived the winter,
withered but green, sharp-smelling
on my hand. Am I that tenacious,
or just terrified of change?

Restless under the kitchen lamp,
you study seed catalogues. When
you finally choose Chinese cabbage,
black radishes, three kinds of corn,
I find I've been holding my breath.

By the time we plant, lilacs are drying,
fragments of dandelion skeleton stream
on the air, catching like snowflakes
in the black dog's fur.

Close to evening, rising from a row
of beans, I see you intent,
planting kernels three to a hill.
We seem like householders now,
committed to this slope, this house,
at least until the corn comes in.

Learning from Moles

I try to touch you,
exposed and awkward
as a mole above ground
that comes up for air, turns
its weak eyes to the night.
Its keen ears hear the cat's tail
lash once before the claws' clasp,
the purring breath.

Spring nights when moles
come out, I find their bodies
on the steps unscarred, dead
of shock I think, snouts still
raised to the wind, front paws
lifted in surrender.

I bury the bodies, so soft
they seem boneless, wishing
they'd stay safe in their tunnels
and caves. Running from you,
I want to go to earth like a mole,
feel my fingernails grow to the shape
of shovels, my nose turn to a rotor.

I'd shape a cave to my dimensions.
Comforted by the dark,
I'd learn from moles,
how to sense without seeing,
how to breathe with less air.

Battered

His words come at me
like fists sometimes.
Drained
after another all-night
argument, how do I
put one foot in front of
the other; how do I
get out of bed?

I think of freedom
as a Southern cruise:
I'd sit lazy in the sun,
wrapped in blankets,
sipping tea until strong enough
to stand on deck in the wind.

My hair, full of spray,
would lift behind me,
each strand like a stripe in a flag.

When I Tell You to Leave

When I tell you to leave,
you lean on the sink watching
your glass fill, and overflow.
You seem lined and hunched
as the old man in the next doorway,
his wallet full of expired licenses,
cracked shoes tied by bits of string.

Ear flaps down, one coat over another,
he shivers in the sun. Once his wife,
waiting up too long, threw his suitcase
out to meet him. Was he old then, or
just your age, fumbling for the handle
as the locks snapped shut on the front
and back doors? Now, late at night
as I hold you, the empty street throbs
like a conveyor belt outside.

Just Looking at the Bones

You ask how am I;
what do you expect?
Empty hangers fill
your side of the closet.
There are spaces
on the shelves that once
held your books. Your toothbrush
is missing, your clarinet, your voice.

If you find deer's legs
torn from the socket
or a few mouse feet
left by the cat, you don't ask
if the animal died.
Just looking at the bones
will tell you, or
looking at my face.

Photograph from Childhood

I keep a photograph his mother sent
when we married still tacked to the wall
where I live alone. In it, he's ten or so,
standing barechested in the sun, shoulders
squared, smile sure under an Indian headdress.

His cheeks are round but his body's thin
and muscular. Over his heart I can see
the hollow like a shell I held to my ear.
His pants are new, bunched at the waist
and covering his shoes.

The way he stands, arms loose
at his sides, I know he's happy
there on the lawn in front of plants
I can't identify and sand dunes
like snowdrifts bordering Lake Michigan.

His mother is behind the camera,
father probably away; their shadows
don't show in the picture. The boy's eyes
are so clear it seems he's never woken
to an argument, or the rattle of windows
as his father slammed the door of the thin-walled
summer house. Sometime in the future I know
he woke to those sounds, thought he must be
dreaming; then, still drowsy, heard his mother's
sobbing, thought it came from his own silent mouth.

3   Notes for a Dark Winter

Notes for a Dark Winter

1

Try not to listen to the wind.
Turn up the radio and when
the power goes, learn to play
the flute, learn to sing
in several languages, concentrate
on the cyrillic alphabet fading in
and out as the lantern you read by
sways in the draft.

2

In the siege of Leningrad,
remember, there was no heat
and by the end one was lucky
to get a potato a day.
Apartments were full of cold
bodies getting colder,
freezing where they fell.

Many who lived
kept studying with gloves on,
kept practicing their violins,
however clumsily, kept doing
their translations, sharing talk
and hot water round the samovar
after the tea leaves were exhausted.

Penelope

I've been reading the Odyssey
to my daughter; for several nights now
Penelope has ripped out her weaving
and at last Odysseus appears in disguise.
"What kind of disguise, Mom?"—We invent one:
a sheepskin tied under his cloak for a hump.
We've added other details: Penelope has eyestrain,
and weaves a tapestry of lions instead of a shroud.

I close the book for tonight, leaving Odysseus
on the threshold, the old dog cocking his ears,
Penelope poised at the loom. I think how faithful
she is to his memory, how long she's been alone.
I wonder if her silent conversation is all
the sound she needs, if her bed, like mine,
no longer seems too wide.

If you came back tomorrow, how would I
greet you? In the poem Penelope hesitates
before she takes Odysseus in. Will she be happier now?
I wonder if the creatures she's woven will still
prowl her mind at night, will still guard her sleep
with their calm, yellow eyes, now that he sleeps beside her.

Cat

At dusk, the black cat and the gray
walk home on the stone wall
with questioning cries. They've given up
waiting for the orange one,
who never comes.

The house is empty without him.
If you pressed him, he'd purr;
you never had to wonder if he
were bored, depressed, wished
he were somewhere else.

I found him, blood caked
at the corner of his mouth
like a wider, darker tongue.
He'd met death, like life,
with eyes wide open, fearless,
taking it in.

Though I knew the cold,
curled shape I buried
was his body, I still expect him
to slip in the house like the sun,
fur so bright it seemed charged
with all the sunlight he'd slept in,
all the frightened eyes of mice,
rivals' claws, the cries of females
twisting under him. When he stretched,
spaces that seem dark now
filled with sparks of light.

Family Man

My friend comes to the dock,
one son on his shoulders, one
pulling his hand, the others
running ahead. I hardly recognize
his shoulders, his stride, feel
he's betrayed me, cutting the hair
I loved long.

He loosens one child gently, swings
and sets the other down with the gravest
attention. He points out crayfish
in the shallows, cautions the children
to stay close, as we talk above their heads.

If I could make him laugh,
I could see his sharp eyeteeth,
but I feel like a fly he wants
to brush off. All he can talk about
are serious subjects: insulation,
his woodstove, the price of gas.

Waves slap the pilings
with a sound of *loss,   loss.*
The sun disappears; crayfish
in their fragile armor scuttle
to safety under the dock.

The children chase them, shivering.
Their father frowns and lifts each
blue-lipped child from the water.
How tenderly he towels them, running
his hands down their thin legs,
rubbing till they laugh and hop away.
Not long ago, the touch of his hand
could warm my whole body, could stop
the chill I am feeling now.

My Neighbor's Kitchen

The kitchen where we hold our meeting
is large, warm and full of light. We sit
at a round oak table, admiring the grain.
We admire the woodstove, the homemade bread
and the glass jars filled with beans.
I want to find fault, but I'm seduced
by children's paintings and pottery mugs.

The woman who lives here is my idea
of the perfect mother, child on her hip,
stirring a soup that cooks all day.
She has the calm of an earlier time,
or a time I've imagined. I wonder
if she ever cries, gets lonely, longs
for silence. She smiles, "My husband
helps a lot," and serves the soup so
gracefully I wish some would spill.

I'd like to be the child now coming home,
tossing his hat in his mother's lap.
Or, I'd like to live with you in a house
like this, children asleep upstairs.
Our faces, finally together, close
to the round brass lamp, would glow
back at us. But we'd find that the bulge
of the lamp makes a distorted reflection.
It wouldn't be us, with such wide, untroubled
foreheads, such smooth, contented cheeks.

They're Sad, These Kisses

"But it's sadder than that, much, much sadder,
Sad as a branch letting its fruit fall for no one."
—Vicente Aleixandre

They're sad, these kisses
we exchange out of habit,
and cold as a goldfish's mouth
pressed to the side of a fishbowl.
We step away from this brief
connection—we never touch now
beyond this kiss—and a flood
of words I'll never say fills
the growing space between us.

Why try to tell you?
Loneliness, anger would strike
your ears like waves
pounding a beach where no one
comes to listen.

The Dog's Breath

The dog's lips stay parted
to the shape of his last breath
which floats out,
leaving his body still
on the steel table.

I lift my hand from his forehead;
the vet and I step back, as if
to give the breath the chance
to escape by the window
of the small, tiled room.

I unfasten his collar, worn
and damp with sweat. Years
of license tags jingle—
his sound as he ran toward me.

People I love will die
far away: old people
I never visit enough,
friends whose bodies
hurtle over guard rails,
the right last word or touch
never fast enough to catch them.

Learning Not to Love You

One evening I notice that the fields
and trees seem washed of color.
The light, moving west, leaves behind
only a white-green, paler than gray,
that closes like a fist below the horizon
and begins to pierce the darkening sky
with star-shaped holes.

This moment without color is so brief
if I weren't looking hard I'd miss it,
and I realize that for nights now
I haven't noticed you're gone.
Thinking of you, I feel almost as calm
as these colorless fields waiting for night.
Just this way, the nerves in the wrist's stump
finally stop remembering the missing hand.

Immune to Spring

I'm immune to spring; May's just a month
to change snow tires, plant the garden,
paint the house. But the grass in the lower field
is a green I've never seen before—deeper
and softer—I could sleep out there
all night. The lilacs' buds rise like torches
and the bloodroot explodes its white stars
out of dead leaves.

Half the men in the restaurant
look like someone I've loved.
The daffodils on the table
seem so much like curls of butter
I could put them on bread.

The Concord String Quartet Plays Rutland High

At night, high school corridors keep
a smell of chalk, apathy and sweat;
troubled shapes seem to hover behind
the guidance counselor's door.

The famous string quartet, playing
the auditorium, is accompanied by
banging radiators, and—disembodied
but empathic—a martial piano, thuds,
cheers from a gymnastic meet downstairs.

Someone's forgotten the houselights,
and I feel pinned under them, captive
in a high school assembly, wondering:
When will I see him again? I watch heads
nodding in time or in sleep, wonder if
they dream of their work, their cars,
someone they love.

The radiators still bang, but the musicians
hear only the music, and it seems as if
they've become one body, four bows moving
in unison over strings and shining wood.
The music—presto now, with feeling—
spins a filament that catches and lifts me
until I swing like a spider starting a new web,
falling free yet suspended from a drag-line
that's all but invisible in this light.

French Class

The teacher shook the chalk in her palm
like a gambler ready to throw the dice.
She wore a man's watch with a broad
leather band, a man's corduroy jacket,
a white sport shirt open at the neck.
She pinioned us each with her eyes,
hard and bright as the turquoise
in her belt. Rolling the chalk in thin,
strong fingers, she'd recite, her mouth
making French shapes we tried in vain
to imitate, her voice low, thrilling
as an actor's.

A graduate of the Sorbonne,
she could not have loved our minds,
filled with nothing but boys we scarcely saw,
the size of our own breasts, which way
to curl our hair. We wondered why
she stayed year after year, watching
our thighs bared under gym tunics,
perhaps loving the way our upturned faces
waited to be touched by her passion
for Baudelaire, Verlaine, Rimbaud.

We repeated after her, "Luxe,
calme, et volupté," and blushed
without knowing why as her eyes
fixed on our lips awkwardly forming
the sensuous sounds. Lonely—
we never thought of a teacher as lonely—
but all she had was one room, her books,
a voice as strong and caressing as hands
moulding clay, yet sharp as a chisel,
making such deep marks in my mind
that now when I read Baudelaire
it is her sound that touches me.

Marina Tsvetayeva

"Perhaps the greatest victory is
over time and gravity."
——Marina Tsvetayeva

In a small south Russian town,
out of money, out of food,
she trades her silver rings
for a rope she weighs in her hand,
knots to a beam.

The arc of her feet
kicking away the chair
inscribes for the last time:
bare room, muddy floor,
end of a loaf left for her son,
August asters drying in a jar.

Her kick is as sure
as her fingers guiding a pen,
as the noose around her neck
taking her past that room
to the landscape she steadily imagined;
the golden mountains of Russian folklore
turn transparent as she passes through.

Mandelstam

In spirit, he strolls the narrow streets
of a town like Florence, dawn wind
fanning his long, loose coat and a sheaf
of papers under his arm. He walks with
head upturned to watch a bundle of wood
winched up a housefront, a woman
in a low-cut blouse plumping pillows,
a child in a nightdress staring back.

Burying his nose in a funeral wreath,
he takes a lily for his buttonhole.
At the fruit market, he juggles three
purple, silver-tinged, translucent plums
and bites the ripest. The wind tugs
at the sheaf of papers, catches them,
whirls them like a flock of homing pigeons
just released. The papers, which are poems,
slip under doors, over transoms, in windows,
and settle on all the sleeping heads.

In reality, the city where he walks
is very cold; the wind carries knives.
He's short of breath and shivering,
but there's no warm place to sit down.
Someone in good shoes and a warm coat
echoes his footfalls. There are no plums,
but if there were, he could not buy one.
Curtains fall into place as he passes; eyes
like surgeons' probes hunt for his thoughts.
He carries no papers; his poems are hidden
in saucepans, in trunks, in his wife's memory,
and they come to him as sounds on the cold wind.
His lips keep moving as he walks, recording
lines, storing them safe in his mind.

In prison, half-mad, close to death,
his lips still moved as if he knew
that someday the poems, hidden as if
in hibernation, would stir like crickets,
like spring peepers, opening their throats,
finding their voices in the first warm nights.
As if he heard under cold streets, below
the frost-line, earth pulsing louder
than the tread of marching feet.

Barn Swallows

First swallows—May 2, 1980—he marks
with the soft wide point of a carpenter's pencil
on the barn wall. He has to stoop to write
at the foot of the list he began in '27
when the swallows came back after the flood.

This year, two birds have the barn
to themselves, finding an old nest
attached like a balcony to a beam.
Sometimes the wind rattles the barn door,
open now in all weather, and the old man
thinks he hears the cows brushing the chains
of their milking stalls. They're gone now:
Butterfly, Number 7, the Old Lady,
and all the ones without names.

Every morning he wakes at four,
like a mother sensing a child
about to cry, and every morning remembers
they've gone. The shapes in the misty fields
turn out to be boulders in the sun.
He might sleep late, but instead, in his nightshirt,
he watches a pair of swallows, their breasts
red-gold like the sunrise, soar straight up
on a single cry, just for the joy of it,
then swoop suicidally close to the ground.

The old man lays kindling in the cookstove,
fills the kettle and puts a few potatoes
in the oven to bake for lunch. The match
he scrapes on metal bursts in the dim kitchen
like the geranium on the sill just coming
into bloom, or like the breasts of swallows
rising red-gold in the red-gold light.

The Amaranthine Desert

Hiking the amaranthine desert, I see
the setting sun has turned the dust pink.
The sun still shines; it sets for hours.
The membranes of my mouth turn to crusts.
Each speck of sand on my skin
has the weight of a stone.

Amaranth: imaginary flower
that never fades; from the Greek roots
for flower, for wither, for quench;
reddish purple, "purple heart flower."

The small bushes of the desert
rise like trees. Far off,
I hear a waterfall, though I cannot
see a stream. I shift my pack
and keep walking. The blisters on my feet
swell to balloons. I think of flowers
in the desert, of the word quench.
The sound of the waterfall is far off,
but it is closer.

Dark Mission

"I have such a dark mission, loving you."
      —Vicente Aleixandre

Visiting your house for the first time,
uninvited, I stand outside in the dark,
holding my gift, watching the lighted windows
of what must be the kitchen where at last
you appear, and test the coffee pot with your palm
as gently as you'd touch a woman's cheek.
You seem tired and restless, stripping off
your sweater and pacing the length of the room,
shaking your head as if to loosen thoughts
that are lodged there. I love to watch you,
hidden behind the shaggy bushes like a spy.

The gift I bring is getting too heavy
to hold much longer; like the light hid
under the bushel, it threatens to ignite.
I hesitate to offer something unworthy
of you, even ugly. You're beautiful for a man,
as you stare at the dark not seeing me,
or thinking of me, films of your own invention
unreeling in your mind. What can I give
that would suit you? In the end, nothing
but my presence now knocking at the door.

The smile I offer hovers between us,
like a hummingbird that moves so fast
it becomes a blur of wings. Your lips
pull back from your teeth, in what I
think is a grimace. I want to be the porch
we're standing on, until I notice how
doubt, annoyance, your fear of love
begin to escape through your teeth like
steam, leaving you free to let me in.